Contents

Introduction

Keeping your baby's toes cosy and warm is important – and it has never been such fun! These projects might be small but there is plenty of scope for creativity when making them.

Many people take up their hooks for the first time when there is a baby on the way. If you are a novice, making baby garments is a great way to learn a new craft – and baby slippers and booties, being particularly tiny, are relatively quick to make.

Each project has clear instructions and colour photographs to help you achieve perfect results. In addition, a handy techniques section explains all the basic skills needed. If you are an experienced crocheter, there should be plenty to interest you, but even if you are a beginner, then this booklet is a great place to start.

Simple shoes

Quick and easy to crochet, these pretty pram shoes can be
made in a range of colours to match any special outfit or occasion.
The straps will help to keep them on your baby's feet.

SIZE
To fit sizes 0–3 [3–6:6–9:9–15]
months. See size guide on page 40.

TENSION
20 sts and 22 rows to 4in (10cm),
measured over rows of double
crochet, using 4mm hook. Use a
larger or smaller hook if necessary
to obtain correct tension.

**MATERIALS AND
EQUIPMENT**
• 1 x 50g ball Artesano Superwash
  Merino DK yarn in shade 5769
  Baby Lavender
• 4mm (UK8:USG-6) crochet hook
• Tapestry needle
• 2 sets of snap fasteners

SOLE (MAKE 2)

Foundation chain: Make 9[11:13:15]ch.

Round 1: 1dc in 2nd ch from hook, 2dc in next ch, 1dc in next ch, 1htr in each of next 2[3:4:5] ch, 1tr in each of next 2[3:4:5]ch, 7tr in last ch; do not turn but work back along opposite side of foundation chain as follows: 1tr in each of next 2[3:4:5]ch, 1htr in each of next 2[3:4:5]ch, 1dc in next ch, 2dc in next ch, 1dc in next ch, join with sl st in 1st dc of round (23[27:31:35] sts).

Round 2: 3ch (counts as 1tr), 2tr in each of next 3 sts, 1tr in each of next 5[7:9:11] sts, 2tr in each of next 3 sts, 3tr in next st, 2tr in each of next 3 sts, 1tr in each of next 5[7:9:11] sts, 2tr in each of next 3 sts, join with sl st to 3rd of 3ch at beg of round (38[42:46:50] sts).

Cut yarn and fasten off.

UPPER (MAKE 2)

Foundation chain: Make 26[30:34:38]ch; join with sl st to 1st ch to make a ring.

Round 1: 1ch (does not count as st), 1dc in 1st ch, 1dc in each of next 9[11:13:15] ch, 2dc in each of next 2ch, 1dc in each of next 2ch, 2dc in each of next 2ch, 1dc in each of next 10[12:14:16]ch, sl st in 1st dc (30[34:38:42] sts).

Round 2: 1ch, 1dc in 1st st, 2dc in next st, 1dc in each of next 8[10:12:14] sts, (2dc in next st, 1dc in next st) twice, 2dc in each of next 2 sts, (1dc in next st, 2dc in next st) twice, 1dc in each of next 8[10:12:14] sts, 2dc in next st, 1dc in last st; join with sl st to 1st dc of round (38[42:46:50] sts).

Work 3[4:5:6] rounds of dc without further shaping; fasten off but do not cut yarn.

> **TIP**
> For an interesting effect, when joining the sole and upper parts of the shoe, you could work the round of slip stitches in a contrasting colour.

MAKING UP

To join sole and upper, with wrong sides together, work 1ch into same place as last st on upper and join with sl st to last st worked on sole, then continue by working 1sl st in each pair of stitches around perimeter; cut yarn and fasten off.

Strap of left shoe

Starting at centre back, count 5[6:7:8] sts to the right of this point along top edge of shoe and mark this stitch.

Foundation row: Make 24[27:30:33]ch, then work 1dc into marked st and 1dc into each of next 9[11:13:15] sts along top edge; turn.

Row 1: 1ch, 1dc in each dc of previous row, then 1dc in each ch to end; cut yarn and fasten off.

Strap of right shoe

Starting at centre back, count 5[6:7:8] sts to the right of this point along top edge of shoe and join yarn to this stitch.

Foundation row: Work 1dc into marked st and 1dc into each of next 9[11:13:15] sts along top edge; turn.

Row 1: Make 25[28:31:32]ch, work 1dc in 2nd ch from hook, 1dc in each ch, then 1dc in each dc of previous row; cut yarn and fasten off.

Finishing

Weave in yarn ends on straps. Attach snap fasteners at ends of straps, following the manufacturer's instructions to fix them securely to the fabric.

TIP
For larger sizes – and for any baby who has started to walk – it is advisable to add non-slip soles.
For instructions, see page 40.

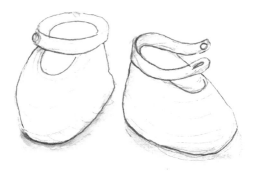

Teddy bear slippers

Soft and snug, with a pair of friendly teddy-bear faces, these alpaca slippers are not only warm but make fun little characters to talk to and play with.

MATERIALS AND EQUIPMENT
- 1 x 50g ball Artesano 100% Alpaca yarn in shade NZ95 Caramel Twist (A)
- 1 x 50g ball Artesano 100% Alpaca yarn in shade SFN10 Cream (B)
- Small amount of DK or tapestry yarn in black
- 3.5mm (UK9:USE-4) crochet hook
- Stitch marker
- Tapestry needle
- 2 small domed buttons with shank, black
- 4 small, round, flat buttons, black
- Sewing needle
- Black sewing thread

TENSION
20 sts and 22 rows to 4in (10cm), measured over rows of double crochet, using 3.5mm hook. Use a larger or smaller hook if necessary to obtain correct tension.

SIZE
To fit sizes 6–9 [9–12:12–15] months. See size guide on page 40.

SLIPPER (MAKE 2)

Foundation chain: Using yarn A, make 36[40:44]ch.

Foundation row: 1dc in 2nd ch from hook, 1dc in each ch to end (35[39:43] sts).

Row 1: 1ch (does not count as st), 1dc in 1st dc, (1ch, miss 1dc, 1dc in next dc) 17[19:21] times.

Row 2: 1ch, 1dc in each dc and 1-ch sp to end.

Row 3: 1ch, 1dc in 1st dc, 1dc in each of next 22[25:28]dc; turn.

Row 4: 1ch, 1dc in 1st dc, 1dc in each of next 10[12:14]dc; turn and place marker in base of last st worked.

Instep

Work 8[10:12] rows of dc on these centre 11[13:15] sts; cut yarn and fasten off.

Upper

Row 1: With RS facing, rejoin yarn to marked st and work 1ch then 8[10:12]dc along side of instep, 1dc in each dc along top, 8[10:12]dc down opposite side and 1dc in each dc to end.

Row 2: 1ch, 1dc in each dc to end (51[59:67] sts).

Rep row 2 a further 6[8:10] times.

Sole

Row 1: 1ch, 1dc in 1st dc, (dc2tog over next 2dc, 1dc in each of next 20[24:28]dc, dc2tog over next 2dc, 1dc in next dc) twice (47[55:63] sts).

Row 2: 1ch, 1dc in 1st dc, (dc2tog over next 2dc, 1dc in each of next 18[22:26]dc, dc2tog over next 2dc, 1dc in next dc) twice (43[51:59] sts).

Row 3: 1ch, 1dc in 1st dc, (dc2tog over next 2dc, 1dc in each of next 16[20:24]dc, dc2tog over next 2dc, 1dc in next dc) twice (39[47:55] sts).

Row 4: 1ch, 1dc in 1st dc, (dc2tog over next 2dc, 1dc in each of next 14[18:22]dc, dc2tog over next 2dc, 1dc in next dc) twice (35[42:51] sts).

Row 5: 1ch, 1dc in 1st dc, (dc2tog over next 2dc, 1dc in each of next 12[16:20]dc, dc2tog over next 2dc, 1dc in next dc) twice; cut yarn and fasten off.

MAKING UP

Stitch underfoot and back seams. Starting at centre back, thread a tie cord through eyelet holes just below top edge of each shoe.

FACE (MAKE 2)

Using yarn B, make a magic loop and work 1ch (to secure ring), then 9dc into ring; join with a sl st to 1st dc and pull up tail of yarn to close hole in centre.

Round 1: 1ch, 2dc in each dc of previous round (18 sts).

Round 2: 1ch, 1dc in 1st dc, 2dc in next dc, (1dc in next dc, 2dc in next dc) 8 times (27 sts).

Round 3: 1ch, 1dc in each dc of previous round.

Round 4: 1ch, 1dc in each of first 2dc, 2dc in next dc, (1dc in each of next 2dc, 2dc in next dc) 8 times; cut yarn and fasten off, leaving a tail of yarn.

EAR (MAKE 4)

Using yarn B, make a magic loop and work 1ch (to secure ring), then 9dc into ring; join with a sl st to 1st dc and pull up tail of yarn to close hole in centre.

Row 1: 1ch, 1dc in 1st st, 2dc in each of next 6 sts, 1dc in next st; cut yarn and fasten off.

Row 2: Join A to 1st dc of previous round and work 1ch, 1dc in each dc of previous round; cut yarn and fasten off.

CORD (MAKE 2)

Using yarn A, make 65ch and work 1sl st in 2nd ch from hook then 1sl st in each ch to end; cut yarn and fasten off.

TO FINISH

Stitch the face firmly to the front of the slipper by oversewing the edges, stitch by stitch, using the tail of yarn, then stitch two ears to edges of face, oversewing the lower edge of each ear to the edge of the face.

Weave in remaining yarn ends. Insert the shank of the button into the central hole on the face and stitch securely in place on the inside of the shoe. Stitch on two small black buttons for eyes. Thread the tapestry needle with a length of black yarn and embroider the mouth: one straight stitch going down from the base of the nose and a curved line of backstitch following the lines of the crocheted stitches. Thread the cord through the eyelet holes on each slipper, starting and ending at centre back, then tie the ends in a bow.

TIP
Buttons must be attached securely; if you prefer, you could embroider the bear's features instead, using black yarn.

Cowboy boots

Wild West-style booties are just the thing for a tiny tenderfoot. Here they are made in a stylish combination of grey-green and cream, although you could choose any two contrasting colours.

BOOTIE (MAKE 2)

Foundation chain: Using yarn A, make 36[40:44]ch.

Foundation row (RS): 1dc in 2nd ch from hook, 1dc in each ch to end (35[39:43] sts).

Row 1: 1ch, 1dc in 1st dc, 1dc in each dc to end; cut A and join in B on last st. Using B, rep row 1 a further 6[8:10] times.

Next row: 1ch, 1dc in 1st dc, 1dc in each of next 2dc, (dc2tog over next 2dc, 1dc in each of next 2dc) 8[9:10] times (27[30:33] sts).

Next row: 1ch, 1dc in each st. Rep last row twice more.

Next row: 1ch, 1dc in each of first 3 dc, (2dc in next dc, 1dc in each of next 2dc) 8[9:10] times (35[39:43] sts).

Next row: 1ch, 1dc in each st; fasten off and place marker in last st; turn.

Instep

With RS facing, miss first 12[13:14]dc and join yarn A to next dc.

Row 1: 1ch, 1dc in 1st dc, 1dc in each of next 10[12:14]dc; turn.

Row 2: 1ch, 1dc in each of these centre 11[13:15]dc, inserting hook into front loop only.

Row 3: 1ch, 1dc in each dc of prev row. Rep row 3 a further 5[7:9] times.

Next row: 1ch, dc2tog over next dc, 1dc in next 7[9:11]dc, dc2tog over next 2 sts (9[11:13] sts).

Next row: 1ch, 1dc in each dc to end.

Next row: 1ch, dc2tog over next dc, 1dc in next 5[7:9]dc, dc2tog over next 2 sts (7[9:11] sts).

Row 4: 1ch, 1dc in 1st dc, (dc2tog over next 2dc, 1dc in each of next 13[17:21]dc, dc2tog over next 2dc, 1dc in next dc) twice (33[41:49] sts).
Row 5: 1ch, 1dc in 1st dc, (dc2tog over next 2dc, 1dc in each of next 11[15:19]dc, dc2tog over next 2dc, 1dc in next dc) twice; cut yarn and fasten off.

Tongue

With RS facing and toe towards you, return to row 2 of the upper and the unworked back loops, on the RS of the work.
Miss the first 3 loops and rejoin yarn A to next loop.
Row 1: 1ch, 1dc in 1st loop, 1dc in each of next 4[6:8] loops; turn (5[7:9] sts).
Row 2: 1ch, 1dc in each dc of prev row.
Rep row 2 a further 3[5:7] times.
Next row: 1ch, 2dc in 1st st, 1dc in each dc to last st, 2dc in last dc; turn (7[9:11] sts).
Next row: 1ch, 1dc in each of first 1[2:3] dc, 1htr in next st, 1tr in next st, 1dtr in next st, 1tr in next st, 1htr in next st, 1dc in each st to end of row; fasten off.
Repeat for other bootie.

LOOP

Using yarn A, make 4ch.
Foundation row (RS): 1dc in 2nd ch from hook, 1dc in each ch to end (3 sts).
Row 1: 1ch, 1dc in 1st dc, 1dc in each dc to end.
Rep row 1 a further 10 times.
Cut yarn and fasten off.

MAKING UP

Stitch underfoot and back seams. Stitch the tongue firmly to the front of the bootie by oversewing the edges, stitch by stitch, using the tail of yarn; then stitch the two ends of the loop to the top of the bootie, over the back seam.

Next row: 1ch, 1dc in each dc to end; fasten off.
With RS facing, rejoin yarn to marked st and work 1ch, 1dc in each of next 12[13:14]dc, 8[10:12]dc evenly spaced up side of instep, 1dc in each dc along top edge, 8[10:12]dc down other side of instep and 1dc in each dc to end of row (47[55:63] sts).
Row 2: 1ch, 1dc in each dc of prev row.
Rep row 2 a further 4[6:8] times; cut A and join in B on last st.

Sole

Row 1: Using yarn B, 1ch, 1dc in each of next 21[25:29]dc, dc2tog over next 2dc, 1dc in next dc, dc2tog over next 2dc, 1dc in each of next 21[25:29]dc (45[53:61] sts).
Row 2: 1ch, 1dc in 1st dc, (dc2tog over next 2dc, 1dc in each of next 17[21:25]dc, dc2tog over next 2dc, 1dc in next dc) twice (41[49:57] sts).
Row 3: 1ch, 1dc in 1st dc, (dc2tog over next 2dc, 1dc in each of next 15[19:23]dc, dc2tog over next 2dc, 1dc in next dc) twice (37[45:53] sts).

Lacy sandals

Light, crisp cotton is the perfect choice for a baby's summer shoes. These ones are suitable for everyday wear but special enough for a christening or other dress-up event.

SIZE

To fit sizes 0–3[3–6:6–9] months. See size guide on page 40.

TENSION

22 sts and 34 rows to 4in (10cm), measured over rows of double crochet, using 3.5mm hook. Use a larger or smaller hook if necessary to obtain correct tension.

MATERIALS AND EQUIPMENT

- 1 x 50g ball Rowan Siena 4-ply yarn in shade 0651 White
- 3.5mm (UK9:USE-4) crochet hook
- Stitch marker
- Tapestry needle
- 48in (1.2m) narrow white ribbon or cotton tape
- Sewing needle and white thread

UPPER (MAKE 2)

Foundation row: Make 2ch; work 3dc in 2nd ch from hook; turn (3 sts).

Row 1: 1ch (does not count as st), 2dc in each dc of previous row; turn (6 sts).

Row 2: 1ch, 2dc in each dc of previous row; turn (12 sts).

Row 3: 3ch (counts as 1tr), 1tr in same place, (1tr in next dc, 2tr in next dc) 5 times, 1tr in last dc; do not turn but work 11dc along straight edge, working last 3dc in 3ch at start of row; turn (21 sts).

Row 4: 1ch, 1dc in each of 11dc on straight edge; turn.

Row 5: 1ch, 1dc in each of first 5dc on straight edge, miss 1dc, 1dc in each of next 5dc; do not turn.

Sides

Round 1: Work 2 more dc in last st worked and place marker in first of these, then 1dc in 3rd of 3ch and in each of 17tr around curved edge of toe, 2dc in same place as 1st dc of row 5, 26[30:34]ch; join with sl st to marked st (48[52:56] sts).

Round 2: 1ch, 1dc in each dc of previous round.

Rep round 2 a further 1[2:3] time(s).

Next round: 1ch, 1dc in each of next 9dc, (dc2tog) twice, 1dc in each of next 20[22:24]dc, (dc2tog) twice, 1dc in each of next 11[13:15]dc; join with sl st to 1st dc of round (44[48:52] sts).

Next round: 1ch, 1dc in each of next 8dc, (dc2tog) twice, 1dc in each of next 32[36:40]dc; join with sl st to 1st dc of round (42[46:50] sts).

Cut yarn and fasten off.

SOLE (MAKE 2)

Foundation chain: Make 11[13:15]ch.

Round 1: 1dc in 2nd ch from hook, 2dc in next ch, 1dc in next ch, 1htr in each of next 3[4:5]ch, 1tr in each of next 3[4:5]ch, 7tr in last ch; do not turn but work back along opposite side of foundation chain as follows: 1tr in each of next 3[4:5]ch, 1htr in each of next 3[4:5]ch, 1dc in next ch, 2dc in next ch, 1dc in next ch, join with sl st in 1st dc of round (27[31:35] sts).

Round 2: 3ch (counts as 1tr), 2tr in each of next 3 sts, 1tr in each of next 6[8:10]

sts, 2tr in each of next 3 sts, 3tr in next st, 2tr in each of next 3 sts, 1tr in each of next 6[8:10] sts, 2tr in each of next 3 sts, 1tr in next dc, join with sl st to 3rd of 3ch at beg of round (42[46:50] sts).

Fasten off but do not cut yarn. Line up centre back of upper with centre back of sole and work 1sl st in each pair of sts to join, inserting hook in back loop only of each st.

BACK CASING

Foundation row: With RS facing, counting from straight edge of toe cap, miss 5[6:7] ch on upper edge, join yarn to next st and work 1ch, 1dc in same st and 1dc in each of next 15[17:19]ch; turn (16[18:20] sts).

Row 1: 1ch, 1dc in each dc of prev row. Rep row 1 a further 4 times.

Cut yarn and fasten off.

TAB

Foundation chain: Make 9ch.

Foundation row: 1dc in 2nd ch from hook, 1dc in each of next 8ch (8 sts).

Row 1: 1ch, 1dc in each dc of prev row. Cut yarn and fasten off.

MAKING UP

Fold back casing to RS and oversew sts on last row to base of casing. Cut ribbon or tape in half and thread one piece through casing on each shoe. Weave in all remaining yarn ends.

> ### TIP
> These little shoes would make a lovely gift for a new baby. You could use any coloured ribbon you like to suit the new arrival.

Watermelon booties

Fruity and fun, these pull-on booties have ties to secure them around the ankle and styling that will make you smile.

LEG AND INSTEP (MAKE 2)

Foundation chain: Using yarn A, make 27[31:35]ch.

Row 1: 1dc in 2nd ch from hook, 1dc in each ch to end (26[30:34] sts).

Row 2: 1ch (does not count as st), 1dc in each ch to end.

Rep row 2 a further 8[10:12] times.

Next row: 1ch, 1dc in 1st st, (1ch, miss 1 st, 1dc in next st) 12[14:16] times, 1dc in last st.

Next row: 1ch, 1dc in each dc and ch sp of previous row.

Next row: 1dc in 1st st, 1dc in each of next 16[18:20] sts; turn.

Next row: 1ch, 1dc in 1st st, 1dc in each of next 7 sts; turn (8dc).

Place marker in base of last st worked, then rep previous row 10[12:14] times. Fasten off.

Remove marker and rejoin yarn to same place, then work 11[13:15] sts evenly

SIZE

To fit size 0–3[3–6:6–9] months. See size guide on page 40.

TENSION

24 sts and 30 rows to 4in (10cm), measured over rows of double crochet using 3mm hook. Use a larger or smaller hook if necessary to obtain correct tension.

MATERIALS AND EQUIPMENT

- 1 x 50g ball Rowan 4-ply cotton yarn in shade 133 Cheeky (A)
- 1 x 50g ball Rowan 4-ply cotton yarn in shade 135 Fennel (C)
- Small amount of Rowan 4-ply cotton yarn in shade 113 Bleached (B)
- 3mm (UK11:USC-2/D3) crochet hook
- Stitch marker
- Tapestry needle
- Black embroidery thread

TIP

As an alternative to the crocheted cords, you could use ⅜in (10mm) wide ribbon instead.

along side of instep, inserting hook into row ends, then 1dc in each of 8 sts along top, 11[13:15]dc down opposite edge and 1dc in each of 9[11:13] sts on other side (48[56:64] sts).

Cut yarn and join in B.

Next row: 1ch, 1dc in each dc to end; turn. Rep previous row once more, then cut yarn and join in C.

Next row: 1ch, 1dc in each dc to end; turn. Rep previous row 2[3:4] times. Cut yarn and fasten off.

SOLE (MAKE 2)

Foundation chain: Using yarn C, make 8[9:10]ch.

Row 1: 1dc in 2nd ch from hook, 1dc in each ch to end; turn (7[8:9] sts).

Row 2: 1ch, 2dc in first dc, 1dc in each of next 5[6:7]dc, 2dc in last dc; turn (9[11:13] sts).

Row 3: 1ch, 2dc in first dc, 1dc in each of next 7[8:9]dc, 2dc in last dc; turn (11[13:15] sts).

Row 4: 1ch, 1dc in each dc to end; turn. Rep row 4 a further 16[20:24] times.

Next row: 1ch, dc2tog over first 2dc, 1dc in each of next 7[8:9]dc, dc2tog over last 2dc (9[11:13] sts).

Next row: 1ch, dc2tog over first 2dc, 1dc in each of next 5[6:7]dc, dc2tog over last 2dc (7[9:11] sts).

Cut yarn and fasten off.

FLAT CORD (MAKE 2)

Make 2ch, then work 1dc in 1st of these 2ch; *turn work clockwise away from you so that second loop of dc just worked is uppermost, insert hook through both loops of this st and work 1dc, rep from * 80[84:88] times, or until cord is long enough to fit around leg and tie in a bow.

MAKING UP

Stitch back seam, then stitch upper to sole. Thread tapestry needle with embroidery thread and embroider a scattering of watermelon seeds on the instep of each bootie.

Starting at the centre front, thread one flat cord through the eyelet holes in each bootie and tie the ends in a neat bow.

Button boots

Perfect for cold-weather outings in the pushchair or cosy storytelling sessions on the sofa, these boots are crocheted in a ridged stitch, making them extra thick and warm.

RIGHT BOOTIE

Leg and instep

Foundation chain: Make 35[39:43]ch.

Row 1: 1dc in 2nd ch from hook, 1dc in each ch to end (34[38:42] sts).

Row 2: 1ch (does not count as st), 1dc in each ch to end (remembering to insert the hook into the back loop only of each st).

Row 3: 1ch, 1dc in each dc to end.

Row 4: As row 3.

Row 5 (buttonhole): 1ch, 1dc in 1st st, 2ch, miss 2dc, 1dc in each dc to end.

Row 6: 1ch, 1dc in each st to end.

Rep row 6 a further 4[6:8] times.

Next row (buttonhole): 1ch, 1dc in 1st st, 2ch, miss 2dc, 1dc in each dc to end.

Rep row 6 a further 3 times.

Bring opposite edge around to form a cylinder, overlapping the edges, and line up the last 8 sts of the row just worked behind the first 8 sts and proceed as follows: Work 1sl st, inserting hook through back loop of 1st st and the corresponding st behind; do the same with the next 7 pairs of sts (26[30:34] sts).

Next row: 1ch, 1dc in 1st st, 1dc in each of next 4 sts; turn.

Next row: 1ch, 1dc in 1st st, 1dc in each of next 7 sts; turn (8 sts).

Place marker in base of last st worked, then rep previous row 10[12:14] times. Cut yarn and fasten off.

Remove marker and rejoin yarn to same place, then work 11[13:15] sts evenly along side of instep, inserting hook into row ends, then 1dc in each of 8 sts along top, 11[13:15]dc down opposite edge and 1dc in each of first 10[12:14] sts on other side.

Next row: 1ch, 1dc in each of next 23[27:31]dc, (dc2tog over next 2dc) twice, 1dc in each dc to end (48[56:64] sts).

Next row: 1ch, 1dc in each dc to end; turn. Rep previous row a further 4[6:8] times. Cut yarn and fasten off.

SIZE

To fit sizes 6–9[9–12:12–15] months. See size guide on page 40.

TENSION

20 sts and 28 rows to 4in (10cm), measured over rows of double crochet using a 3.5mm hook. Use a larger or smaller hook if necessary to obtain correct tension.

MATERIALS AND EQUIPMENT

- 1 x 50g ball Artesano DK 100% Alpaca yarn in shade CA13 Sweet Pea
- 3.5mm (UK9:USE-4) crochet hook
- Tapestry needle
- 4 fabric-covered buttons

PATTERN NOTE

The attractive ridged pattern is achieved by inserting the crochet hook into the back loops of the stitches.

LEFT BOOTIE
Leg and instep

Foundation chain: Make 35[39:43]ch.

Row 1: 1dc in 2nd ch from hook, 1dc in each ch to end (34[38:42] sts).

Row 2: 1ch (does not count as st), 1dc in each ch to end (remembering to insert the hook into the back loop only of each st).

Row 3: 1ch, 1dc in each dc to end.

Row 4: As row 3.

Row 5 (buttonhole): 1ch, 1dc in each dc to last 3dc, 2ch, miss 2dc, 1dc in last dc.

Row 6: 1ch, 1dc in each st to end.

Rep row 6 a further 4[6:8] times.

Next row (buttonhole): 1ch, 1dc in each dc to last 3dc, 2ch, miss 2dc, 1dc in last dc.

Rep row 6 a further 3 times.

Next row: Sl st in back loop only of 1st 8 sts, then work 1dc in each of next 18[22:26] sts, join last 8 sts and 1st 8 sts of row by working a sl st in each pair of sts, then work 1dc in each of last 2 sts; cut yarn and place a marker in last st worked (26[30:34] sts).

With WS facing, count back along row to 11th st from end and rejoin yarn to this st.

Next row: 1ch, 1dc in 1st st, 1dc in each of next 4 sts; turn.

Next row: 1ch, 1dc in 1st st, 1dc in each of next 7 sts; turn (8 sts).

Rep previous row 10[12:14] times. Cut yarn and fasten off.

Remove marker and rejoin yarn to this place, then with WS facing, work 1dc in each of next 10[12:14]dc, 11[13:15] sts evenly up side of instep, inserting hook into row ends, then 1dc in each of 8 sts along top, and 11[13:15]dc down opposite edge; turn.

Next row: 1ch, 1dc in each of next 23[27:31]dc, (dc2tog over next 2dc) twice, 1dc in each dc to end (48[56:64] sts).

Next row: 1ch, 1dc in each dc to end; turn.

Rep previous row a further 4[6:8] times. Cut yarn and fasten off.

SOLE (MAKE 2)

Foundation chain: Make 8[9:10]ch.

Row 1: 1dc in 2nd ch from hook, 1dc in each ch to end; turn (7[8:9] sts).

Row 2: 1ch, 2dc in first dc, 1dc in each of next 5[6:7]dc, 2dc in last dc; turn (9[11:13] sts).

Row 3: 1ch, 2dc in first dc, 1dc in each of next 7[8:9]dc, 2dc in last dc; turn (11[13:15] sts).

Row 4: 1ch, 1dc in each dc to end; turn. Rep row 4 19[23:27] times.

Next row: 1ch, dc2tog over first 2dc, 1dc in each of next 7[8:9]dc, dc2tog over last 2dc (9[11:13] sts).

Next row: 1ch, dc2tog over first 2dc, 1dc in each of next 5[6:7]dc, dc2tog over last 2dc (7[9:11] sts).

Cut yarn and fasten off.

MAKING UP

Stitch upper to sole.

Stitch buttons in place to correspond with buttonholes.

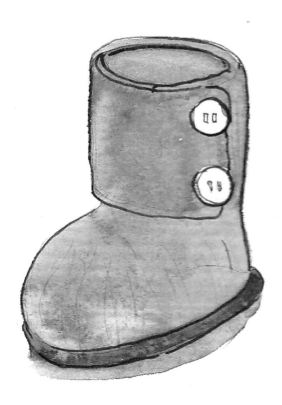

Daisy slippers

**Made in peppermint green and candy pink,
these slippers are simple to make and will appeal
to little girls who like dressing up.**

SIZE
To fit sizes 15–18[18–24:24–36]
months. See size guide on page 40.

TENSION
18 sts and 10 rows to 4in (10cm),
measured over rows of double
crochet, using a 4mm hook.
Use a larger or smaller hook if
necessary to obtain correct tension.

PATTERN PIECES
You will need the following pattern
pieces from the templates:
Sole • cut 2 in soft leather

MATERIALS AND EQUIPMENT
• 1 x 50g ball Rowan Belle Organic
  by Amy Butler DK yarn in shade
  25 Dew (A)
• 1 x 50g ball Rowan Belle Organic
  by Amy Butler DK yarn in shade
  29 Dahlia (B)
• 4mm (UK8:USG-6)
  crochet hook
• Piece of soft leather approximately
  7 x 7in (18 x 18cm)
• Leather punch
• Tapestry needle
• 4 small ball buttons, translucent
• Sewing needle and thread

SOLE (MAKE 2)
Using the templates on pages 46–7, cut
two soles from soft leather and punch
31[35:39] holes, as indicated on the
pattern pieces.
Foundation round: Using yarn A, join yarn
to hole at centre back of sole and work 1ch
(does not count as st), 1dc in same place,
then *1dc in next hole, 2dc in next hole; rep
from * to end; join with sl st to 1st dc and
fasten off (46[52:58] sts).

UPPER (MAKE 2)
Foundation chain: Using yarn A, make
30[36:42]ch; join with sl st to 1st ch to
make a ring.
Round 1: 1ch (does not count as st), 1dc
in 1st ch, 1dc in each of next 11[14:17]ch,
2dc in each of next 2ch, 1dc in each of
next 2ch, 2dc in each of next 2ch, 1dc in
each of next 12[15:18]ch, sl st in 1st dc
(34[40:46] sts).
Round 2: 1ch, 1dc in 1st dc, 1dc in each
of next 13[16:19]dc, 2dc in each of next 2
dc, 1dc in each of next 2dc, 2dc in each of
next 2dc, 1dc in each of next 14[17:20]dc,
sl st in 1st dc (38[44:50] sts).
Round 3: 1ch, 1dc in 1st st, 2dc in next st,
1dc in each of next 12[15:18] sts, (2dc in
next st, 1dc in next st) twice, 2dc in each
of next 2 sts, (1dc in next st, 2dc in next st)
twice, 1dc in each of next 12[15:18] sts,
2dc in next st, 1dc in last st; join with sl st
to 1st dc of round (46[52:58] sts).
Work 2[3:4] rounds of dc without further
shaping; fasten off but do not cut yarn.

DAISY (MAKE 2)

Using yarn B, make 6ch and join with a sl st to 1st ch to make a ring.

Round 1: 1ch (does not count as st), 10dc in ring; join with sl st to 1st dc of round (10 sts).

Round 2: (6ch, sl st into next dc) 10 times; cut yarn, leaving a tail, and fasten off.

FLOWER CENTRE (MAKE 2)

Using yarn A, make a magic loop and work 1ch (does not count as st), 6dc into ring; join with a sl st to 1st dc and pull up tail of yarn to close gap in centre.

Round 1: 1ch (does not count as st), 2dc in each dc of 1st round; join with a sl st to 1st dc; cut yarn, leaving a tail, and fasten off (20 sts).

STRAP (MAKE 2)

Using yarn B, make 15[16:17]ch.

Row 1: 1dc in 6th ch, 1dc in each ch to end.

Cut yarn leaving a tail and fasten off.

MAKING UP

To join the sole and upper, with wrong sides together and beginning at centre back, using yarn B, work 1sl st in each pair of stitches around perimeter, inserting the hook into the back loops only (one loop from upper and one loop from sole); cut yarn and fasten off. On the top edge of each shoe, beginning at centre back, using yarn B, work 1sl st in each stitch, inserting the hook into one loop only on foundation chain; cut yarn and fasten off.

Stitch end of strap to outside of shoe, halfway along side, making sure that the straps are on different sides to create a left and right shoe. Stitch a ball button on the opposite side of each shoe and fasten using the chain loop at the other end of each strap.

For the flower centre, thread the tail of yarn into a tapestry needle and thread through each loop around the edge, then pull up to gather and form a neat ball shape; stitch one flower centre to the centre of each daisy, then stitch one daisy firmly to the front of each shoe. Stitch a ball button to the centre of each, pulling the shank down inside the hole in the flower centre and fasten off securely.

Baseball boots

Sporty and casual in style, these snug-fitting lace-ups are a move away from the more traditional bootie and are great for both baby boys and girls.

SOLE (MAKE 2)

Foundation chain: Using yarn A, make 11[13:15]ch.

Round 1: 3dc in 2nd ch from hook, 1dc in each of next 8[10:12]ch, 6dc in last ch; then, working back along foundation chain, 1dc in each of next 8[10:12]ch, 3dc in last ch, join with sl st to 1st dc of round (28[32:36] sts).

Round 2: 1ch (does not count as st), 2dc in each of first 3dc, 1dc in each of next 8[10:12]dc, 2dc in each of next 6dc, 1dc in each of next 8[10:12]dc, 2dc in each of last 3dc; join with sl st to 1st dc of round (40[44:48] sts).

Round 3: 1ch, 2dc in 1st dc, 1dc in next dc, (2dc in next dc, 1dc in next dc) twice, 1dc in each of next 8[10:12]dc, (2dc in next dc, 1dc in next dc) 6 times, 1dc in each of next 8[10:12]dc, (2dc in next dc, 1dc in next dc) 3 times (52[56:60] sts).

Round 4: 1ch, 1dc in each dc of previous round. Fasten off.

UPPER (MAKE 2)

Foundation chain: Using yarn B, make 31[35:39]ch.

Row 1: 1dc in 2nd ch from hook, 1dc in each ch to end (30[34:38] sts).

Row 2: 1ch, 1dc in each dc of prev row. Rep row 2 a further 1[3:5] time(s).

Next row: 1ch, dc2tog over next 2dc, 1dc in each dc to last 2dc, dc2tog over last 2dc; turn. Rep previous row 3 times more (22[26:30] sts).

Next row: 1ch, 1dc in each dc of prev row.

Edging

Round 1: 1ch, 1dc in 1st dc, 1dc in each of next 20[24:28]dc, 3dc in last dc of row, then 6[8:10]dc down sloping edge, 3[5:7] dc along straight edge, 3dc in 1st ch of foundation ch (place marker in 2nd of these 3dc), 1dc in each of next 28[32:36] ch, 3dc in last ch (place marker in 2nd of these 3dc), 3[5:7]dc along straight edge, 6[8:10]dc up opposite side, 2dc in same place as 1st dc of round (76[84:92] sts). Cut yarn B and fasten off.

Next row: Join yarn C to 1st marked st, then work 1ch, 1dc in each dc of previous row, finishing at 2nd marked st; fasten off.

TONGUE (MAKE 2)

Foundation chain: Using B, make 8[10:12]ch.

Row 1 (RS): 1dc in 2nd ch from hook, 1dc in each ch to end (7[9:11] sts).

Row 2: 1ch, 2dc in 1st dc, 1dc in each dc to last dc, 2dc in last dc (9[11:13] sts).

Row 3: 1ch, 1dc in each dc of prev row. Rep row 3 a further 9[11:13] times.

Next row: 1ch, 2dc in 1st dc, 1dc in each dc to last dc, 2dc in last dc (11[13:15] sts).

Row 14: 1ch, 1dc in each dc of previous row; turn.

Edging

Round 1: 1ch, 1dc in each of first 10[12:14]dc, 2dc in last dc of row, then 12[14:16]dc down side edge, 2dc in 1st ch of foundation ch, 1dc in each of next 5[7:9] ch, 2dc in last ch, 12[14:16]dc up opposite side, 1dc in same place as 1st dc of round, join with a sl st to 1st dc; fasten off (46[54:62] sts).

SIZE

To fit sizes 3–6[6–9:9–12] months. See size guide on page 40.

TENSION

19 sts and 22 rows to 4in (10cm), measured over rows of double crochet using 3.5mm hook. Use a larger or smaller hook if necessary to obtain correct tension.

MATERIALS AND EQUIPMENT

- 1 x 50g ball Artesano Soft Merino Superwash DK yarn in shade 0157 White (A)
- 1 x 50g ball Artesano Soft Merino Superwash DK yarn in shade SFN50 Black (B)
- Small amount of Artesano Superfine 100% Alpaca DK yarn in shade 0178 Peru (C)
- 3.5mm (UK9:USE-4) crochet hook
- Tapestry needle

Toe cap

Row 1: With RS facing, join yarn C to first dc of edging row and work 1ch, 1dc in same place, 1dc in each of next 10dc; fasten off (11[13:15] sts).

Row 2: With RS facing, miss first 2dc of row 1 and join yarn A to next dc, then work 1ch, miss next 2[3:4]dc and work 5dc[5htr:5tr] in next dc, miss next 2[3:4]dc and sl st into next dc; turn.

Row 3: 2dc in each of next 5 sts, miss next unworked dc and sl st into rem dc; turn.

Row 4: 1ch, (2dc in next dc, 1dc in next dc) 5 times, miss next unworked dc, sl st in last st (at end of row 1); do not turn and do not cut yarn.

Join tongue and upper

Round 1: 1dc in each of next 2dc on side of tongue, then on lower edge of upper, insert hook through 1st dc and through next dc on side edge of tongue and work 2dc in same st to join; then working in lower edge of upper only, work 1dc in each of next 28[32:36] sts, then insert hook through last st and through 3rd dc from end of tongue edging and work 2dc, then work 1dc in each of last 2dc on side edge of tongue, 1dc in row end on toe cap and 1dc in each dc around curved end of toe cap (52[56:60] sts).

Round 2: 1ch, 1dc in each dc of previous round; do not cut yarn A but join in C.

Round 3: Using C, 1ch, 1dc in each dc of previous round; cut C and fasten off.

Round 4: Using A, 1ch, 1dc in each dc of previous round.

Join sole and upper

Pin centre back sole to centre back of upper.

Round 1: 1ch; then, inserting hook through one loop each of corresponding sts around edge of upper and edge of sole, work 1dc in each pair of sts to join.
Fasten off.

LACE (MAKE 2)

Using yarn A, make 95[100:105]ch; cut yarn and fasten off.

DISC (MAKE 2)

Foundation chain: Using yarn A, make 4ch.

Round 1: 3ch, 11tr in ring, sl st in top of 3ch.
Cut yarn and fasten off.

MAKING UP

Use yarn ends to reinforce joins where corners of Upper meet edges of Toe Cap. Thread laces through gaps between stitches close to contrast edging on front. Stitch a disc to the outer side of each boot.

Ankle tie shoes

These two-colour shoes in soft alpaca yarn with crossover fronts, ankle ties and pretty flower embellishments are perfect for special occasions.

SIZE
To fit sizes 9–12 [12–15:15–18] months. See size guide on page 40.

SOLE (MAKE 2)
Using the template on page 43, cut two soles from soft leather and punch holes, as indicated on the pattern pieces.

LEFT SHOE
First (left-hand) side
Foundation round: Using 3.5mm hook and yarn A, with WS of sole facing, join yarn to hole at centre back of sole and work 1ch (does not count as st), 1dc in same place, then 2dc in each of next 10[12:14] holes, 3dc in each of next 2 holes, 1dc in next hole; turn (28[32:36] sts).

TIP
This is quite a complex pattern, as it has a number of different elements. Each side is worked separately, in a different coloured yarn, and the sloped edges at the front of each piece, created by increasing stitches on each row, have to be wrapped around and sewn in place, forming a double layer of fabric at the toe. There are also a border and ankle ties to be worked, as well as the flower embellishment. As work progresses, you may find it helpful to refer to the picture of the finished shoes to understand how each one is constructed.

TENSION
22 sts and 34 rows to 4in (10cm), measured over rows of double crochet using 3.5mm hook. Use a larger or smaller hook if necessary to obtain correct tension.

PATTERN PIECES
You will need the following pattern pieces from the templates:
Sole • cut 2 in soft leather.

MATERIALS AND EQUIPMENT
- 1 x 50g ball Artesano 4-ply 100% Alpaca yarn in shade CA13 Sweet Pea (A)
- 1 x 50g ball Artesano 4-ply 100% Alpaca yarn in shade C726 Amarylis (B)
- Small amounts of 4-ply cotton yarn in green, yellow and pink
- 3.5mm (UK9:USE-4) crochet hook
- 2.5mm (UK12:USB-1/C-2) crochet hook
- Tapestry needle
- Offcut of soft leather, approximately 6in (15cm) square
- Leather punch

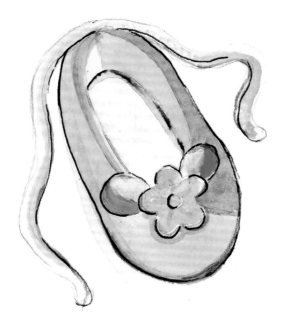

Row 1: 1ch, 2dc in 1st dc, 1dc in each dc to end of row; turn.
Row 2: 1ch, 1dc in 1st dc, 1dc in each dc to last dc, 2dc in last dc; turn.
Rep rows 1 and 2 a further 4[5:6] times (38[44:50] sts).
Fasten off, leaving a tail of yarn for sewing up.

Second (right-hand) side

With RS (underside) of sole facing, join yarn B to centre back hole.
Foundation row: 1ch, 1dc in same hole, 2dc in each of next 9[11:13] holes, 1dc in same hole as 1dc in yarn A, then 1dc in each of next 8dc, at back of work, inserting hook around post of each st; turn (28[32:36] sts).
Row 1: 1ch, 2dc in 1st dc, 1dc in each dc to end of row; turn.
Row 2: 1ch, 1dc in 1st dc, 1dc in each dc to last dc, 2dc in last dc; turn.
Rep rows 1 and 2 a further 4[5:6] times (38[44:50] sts).
Fasten off, leaving a tail of yarn for sewing up.

RIGHT SHOE

For right shoe, follow instructions for left shoe but for first side (which will be the right-hand side), begin with RS of sole facing; then for second side, in yarn B, when you get to the toe work into stitches at the front of the work.

MAKING UP

Stitch back seam on each shoe. On the outside, stitch sloping edge of side worked in yarn B to stitches in yarn A along edge of sole. On the inside, stitch sloping edge worked in yarn A to stitches in B on inside edge of sole. Then stitch straight edges in place on the inside and outside.

BORDER (BOTH SHOES)

Rejoin A to top of centre back seam then with RS facing, work 1ch.
Round 1: 1dc in each of first 2dc, dc2tog over next 2dc, 1dc in each of next 19[23:27]dc, (dc2tog) twice, then holding edges of both sides together where they overlap at centre front, inserting hook

through both layers, work (1dc in next dc) twice, then working through single layer work (dc2tog) twice, 1dc in each of next 19[23:27]dc, dc2tog over next 2dc, 1dc in each of last 2dc; join with sl st to 1st dc of round (54[58:62] sts).
Round 2: 1ch, 1dc in each of first 2dc, dc2tog over next 2dc, 1dc in each of next 17[21:25]dc, htr4tog over next 4dc, 1dc in each of next 17[21:25]dc, dc2tog over next 2dc, 1dc in each of last 2dc; join with sl st to 1st dc of round; fasten off.

TIE (BOTH SHOES)

Row 1: Using 3.5mm hook and yarn A, make 48ch, then work 1sl st into each of 4[6:8]dc of border at centre back of shoe, then 49ch; turn.
Row 2: 1dc in 2nd ch from hook, then 1dc into each ch and sl st of previous row; fasten off.

LEAF (MAKE 4)

Using 2.5mm hook and green yarn, make 6ch.
Round 1: 1dc in 2nd ch from hook, 1htr in each of next 2ch, 1tr in next ch, 3tr in last ch; then, working along opposite edge of foundation ch, 1tr in next ch, 1htr in each of next 2ch, 1dc in next ch, sl st into last ch; fasten off, leaving a tail of yarn.

FLOWER (MAKE 2)

Using 2.5mm hook and yellow yarn, make a magic loop.
Round 1: 1ch, 10dc in ring, join with sl st to 1st dc of round; fasten off and join in pink yarn.
Round 2: 1ch, *(1tr, 2dtr, 1tr) in next ch, 1dc in next ch, rep from * 4 times more, working last dc into 1st ch of round; fasten off, leaving a tail of yarn.

TO FINISH

Stitch a pair of leaves to the centre front of each shoe, along the border, then stitch a flower in the centre of each pair of leaves.

Strappy sandals

Cute and cool, these slippers masquerade as sandals, with handy straps to keep them securely attached to little feet.

SIZE
To fit sizes 12–15[15–18:18–24:24–36] months. See size guide on page 40.

TENSION
18 sts and 10 rows to 4in (10cm), measured over rows of double crochet, using 4mm hook. Use a larger or smaller hook if necessary to obtain correct tension.

PATTERN PIECES
You will need the following pattern pieces from the templates:
Sole • cut 2 in soft leather.

MATERIALS AND EQUIPMENT
- 1 x 50g ball Rowan Belle Organic by Amy Butler DK yarn in shade 023 Bluebell (A)
- 1 x 50g ball Rowan Belle Organic by Amy Butler DK yarn in shade 013 Moonflower (B)
- 4mm (UK8:USG-6) crochet hook
- Piece of soft leather approximately 7 x 7in (18 x 18cm)
- Leather punch
- Tapestry needle
- 4 small buttons, orange
- 4 snap fasteners
- Tools and materials

SOLE AND UPPER (MAKE 2)
Using the templates on pages 44–5, cut two soles from soft leather and punch 27[31:35:39] holes, as indicated on the pattern pieces.

Foundation round: Using 4mm crochet hook and A, join yarn to hole at centre back of sole and work 1ch (does not count as st), 1dc in same place, then 2dc in each hole to end; join with sl st to 1st dc (53[61:69:77] sts).

Round 1: 1ch (does not count as st), 1dc in each dc of previous round; join with sl st in 1st dc.
Rep round 1 2[3:4:5] times more.

Next round: 1 ch, 1dc in 1st dc, 1dc in next dc, dc2tog over next 2dc, 1dc in each of next 14[18:22:26]dc, (dc2tog, 1dc) twice, (2dctog) twice, (1dc, 2dctog) twice, 1dc in each of next 14[18:22:26]dc, dc2tog over next 2 sts, 1dc, sl st to 1st dc (45[53:61:69] sts).
Cut yarn and fasten off.

REAR STRAP OF LEFT SANDAL
With RS facing, starting at centre back and counting dc at centre back as 1st st, count 12 sts to right and rejoin yarn A to this st.

Row 1: Using yarn A, work 1ch (does not count as st), 1dc in same st, 1dc in each of next 2[2:3:3] sts; turn (3[3:4:4] sts).
Row 2: 1ch, 1dc in each dc of prev row.
Rep row 2 a further 10[11:12:13] times more.
Next row: 1ch, miss 1dc, 2[2:3:3]dctog over next 2[2:3:3]dc; cut yarn and fasten off.

FRONT STRAP OF LEFT SANDAL

With RS facing, starting at 12th st, count 6 sts to right, rejoin yarn A to this st and work strap in same way as centre strap but rep row 2 a further 9[10:11:12] times instead.

REAR STRAP OF RIGHT SANDAL

With RS facing, starting at centre back and counting dc at centre back as 1st st, count 10 sts to left and rejoin yarn A to this st, then work centre strap as given for left sandal.

FRONT STRAP OF RIGHT SANDAL

Leave 3dc unworked to left of centre strap, rejoin yarn to next st along and work front strap as given for left sandal.

FLOWER (MAKE 4)

Using yarn B, make 4ch and join with a sl st to 1st ch to make a ring.

Round 1: 1ch (does not count as st), 6dc in ring; join with sl st to 1st dc of round (6 sts).

Round 2: (3ch, sl st into next dc) 6 times; cut yarn, leaving a tail, and fasten off.

MAKING UP

Stitch one flower to the end of each strap and stitch a button in the centre of each. Stitch one half of a snap fastener to the end of each strap on the underside, and the corresponding part of each snap fastener to the opposite side of each strap. Weave in all yarn ends neatly.

Crochet techniques

Crocheting baby slippers and booties is easy and the results are charming. Crochet is very versatile, which means that most of the projects can be made in one piece, without too many seams and with very little finishing off to do.

TOOLS AND MATERIALS

The projects do not require much in the way of tools, but it is advisable to choose good-quality materials for the booties.

Yarns

The projects have been made using a variety of yarns: wool and wool blend yarns produce a soft, supple fabric, while cotton yarns are crisp, easy to work with, and perfect for summer shoes to wear in the pram or pushchair. I prefer to use natural fibres, as these are soft against a baby's skin. Natural yarns tend to be a little more expensive than those made from synthetic fibres, but you only need small quantities, which makes them more affordable. Check the ball band when buying yarn to see if it is machine-washable.

If the specified yarn for any of the patterns is not available, or you decide to substitute another yarn, check the tension (see below) before proceeding with the pattern.

Hooks

Four different hook sizes have been used to make the crocheted booties and slippers: 2.5mm (UK12:USB-1/C-2), 3mm (UK11:USC-2/D-3), 3.5mm (UK9:USE-4) and 4mm (UK8:USG-6). They have been chosen to produce a particular result, and so that the finished shoes or slippers will be the correct size. Once again, it is important to check your tension so that you don't end up with slippers that are too big or too small.

Other materials

Some of the projects require ribbons and buttons; the amounts needed are listed under each project.

FOLLOWING PATTERNS

Before you embark on any project, make sure you have all the tools and materials you require, then read through the pattern from beginning to end to make sure you understand it.

TENSION (GAUGE)

Check your tension (gauge) before you start crocheting to make sure your booties or slippers end up the right size. To check that your tension is correct, work a swatch using the specified yarn and hook, then measure it using a ruler (rather than a tape measure) to count the number of stitches and rows over 4in (10cm). If you have more stitches and rows than the number stated in the pattern, this indicates that you crochet more tightly than the stated tension; your finished item is likely to end up too small, so you will have to try again using a larger hook. If you have fewer stitches, you tend to crochet more loosely, so try again with a smaller hook until you achieve the correct tension.

OTHER EQUIPMENT

• A row counter may be useful for keeping track of how many rows you have worked, while stitch markers are handy to mark certain points in the pattern.

• A blunt tapestry needle is useful for darning in yarn ends and for sewing any seams or joining components.

• You will need a sewing needle and thread for stitching buttons in place. A small pair of scissors will be necessary for cutting yarn.

SAFETY NOTE

Because you are making these booties for very small children and babies, it is vital that you use safe, clean, new materials. Also, think twice before stitching buttons to slippers intended for a very young child if he or she is likely to pull them off. You may prefer to embroider eyes instead, or use another method of fastening the booties.

BASIC CROCHET TECHNIQUES

CHAIN STITCH (CH)

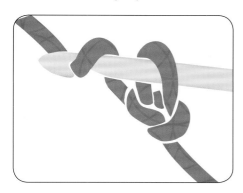

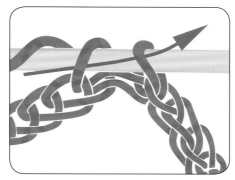

1 Make a slip knot and place it on the hook. With the hook in your right hand and the yarn held in the left hand with your left forefinger controlling the tension, pull the yarn taut. Take the hook under then over the yarn.

2 Use the hook to pull the loop of yarn through the slip knot, then repeat the process, pulling the yarn through the loop on the hook, to form a foundation chain.

SLIP STITCH (SL ST)

1 Push the crochet hook into the top of the next stitch (or through the top of the chain loop when working along the foundation chain), and wrap the yarn around the hook.

2 Use the hook to draw the yarn back through both the top of the stitch and the loop on the hook.

DOUBLE CROCHET (DC)

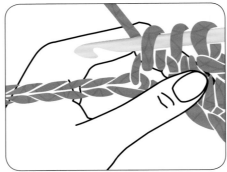

1 Insert the hook into the next stitch, wrap the yarn over the hook and draw the yarn through to the front.

2 Wrap the yarn around the hook again and draw it through both loops on the hook.

HALF TREBLE (HTR)

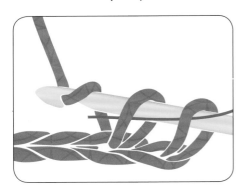

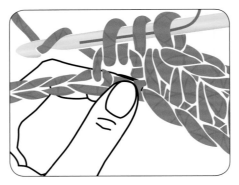

1 Yarn over the hook, then insert the hook into the next stitch. Yarn over and draw the loop through to the front.

2 Yarn over the hook and draw through all three loops on the hook.

TREBLE (TR)

1 Yarn over the hook, then insert the hook into the next stitch.

2 Yarn over the hook and draw the loop through to the front.

3 Yarn over the hook and draw through the first two loops on the hook.

4 Yarn over again and draw through the remaining two loops on the hook.

DOUBLE TREBLE (DTR)

1 Yarn over the hook twice, then insert the hook into the next stitch.

2 Yarn over the hook and draw the loop through to the front.

3 Yarn over the hook and draw through the first two loops on the hook.

4 Yarn over the hook and draw through the next two loops on the hook.

5 Yarn over again and draw through the remaining two loops on the hook.

Foundation chain

To make a flat fabric worked in rows, you must start with a foundation chain. Make a slip knot, then work the number of chains stated in the pattern. When working in the round, the foundation chain is usually joined to create a ring into which you work the first round of stitches.

Magic loop

Instead of beginning with a ring of foundation chains, you can make a loop using the tail of yarn. Crochet the first round of stitches into this, then pull the yarn tail to close the centre up tight.

Working in rows or rounds

To produce a flat crocheted fabric, stitches are worked into the foundation chain, then into the tops of stitches on subsequent rows, turning the work at the end of each row. One or more chains are worked at the beginning of each row in place of the first stitch. When working in rounds, the work is not usually turned (unless stated in the pattern instructions).

Shaping

Each slipper or bootie is shaped to fit a baby's foot; to create the shaping you will need to increase and decrease where the pattern instructs you to do so.

Increases are generally achieved by working two or more stitches into one stitch. Decreasing is usually done by working two or more stitches together or by missing a stitch and working into the next one. Follow the pattern instructions carefully; they will tell you when and how to increase and decrease.

MAKING UP

Most crocheted pieces can be joined by oversewing. In some of the projects, pieces are joined by slipstitching edges together, or by working a row of double crochet into both edges at once – for example, when joining a sole and an upper.

Baby shoe sizes

This chart is intended as a guide to help you decide which size to make for your baby. Just using your baby's age as a guide may not be accurate as he or she may have larger or smaller feet than average. To make sure the booties fit, with wriggle room for little toes, you should measure the length of your baby's feet, using a tape measure, or place them on the template outline on page 42 and make the size indicated on the chart.

UK size	Euro size	US size	approx. age	length (cm)	length (in)
0	16	1	0–3 months	9.5cm	3¾in
1	17	2	3–6 months	10cm	4in
2	18	3	6–9 months	11.5cm	4½in
3	19	4	9–12 months	12.5cm	4⅞in
4	20	5	12–15 months	13cm	5in
5	22	6	15–18 months	14cm	5½in
6	23	7	18–24 months	15cm	6in
7	24	8	24–36 months	16cm	6¼in

Add-on soles

Soles cut from fabric, leather or non-slip material can be stitched on top of the crocheted ones.

ADDING LEATHER SOLES

Leather soles create a firm base, make slippers and booties more hard-wearing, and give a degree of grip – but can still be slippery on polished surfaces. Choose a soft leather and cut out sole shapes using the template on page 42.

There is no need to hem leather as it does not fray. However, for sewing you will need to use a special leather needle, which has a sharp, triangular tip that cuts through the leather. Simply oversew the edges of the sole to the base of your slipper or bootie.

NON-SLIP SOLES

Remember that slippers and booties made from fabric and yarn are not intended for walking. Just like socks, they offer no support and the soles are slippery, especially on hard floors. To create a non-slip sole, you will need to cut out a sole shape from non-slip fabric and stitch this to the base of each slipper or bootie. Non-slip fabrics can be purchased from hardware shops, where they are sold for applying to the underside of table mats and rugs to prevent them from sliding around. Another method is to use a rubber solution specially designed for applying to knitted or crocheted socks and slippers to make them non-slip.

ADDING VELVET SOLES

Needlecord or suedette would also make good fabrics for this purpose.

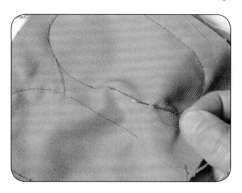

1 Use two pieces of velvet, each at least 8 x 12in (20 x 30cm), and transfer the sole pattern (on page 42) in the desired size twice on to the wrong side of one of the pieces. Place them right sides together, and stitch through both layers, following the lines and leaving a gap of about 1¼–1½in (3–4cm) on one of the straight sides of each sole.

2 Cut out the shapes, adding a ¼in (6mm) seam allowance all round.

3 Turn each sole right sides out, tuck in the seam allowance on the open edge, and slipstitch the folded edges together to close the gap.

4 Slipstitch the edge of each sole to the outer edge at the base of each bootie.

ADD-ON SOLES
You can use these template outlines to make add-on soles as explained on page 40.

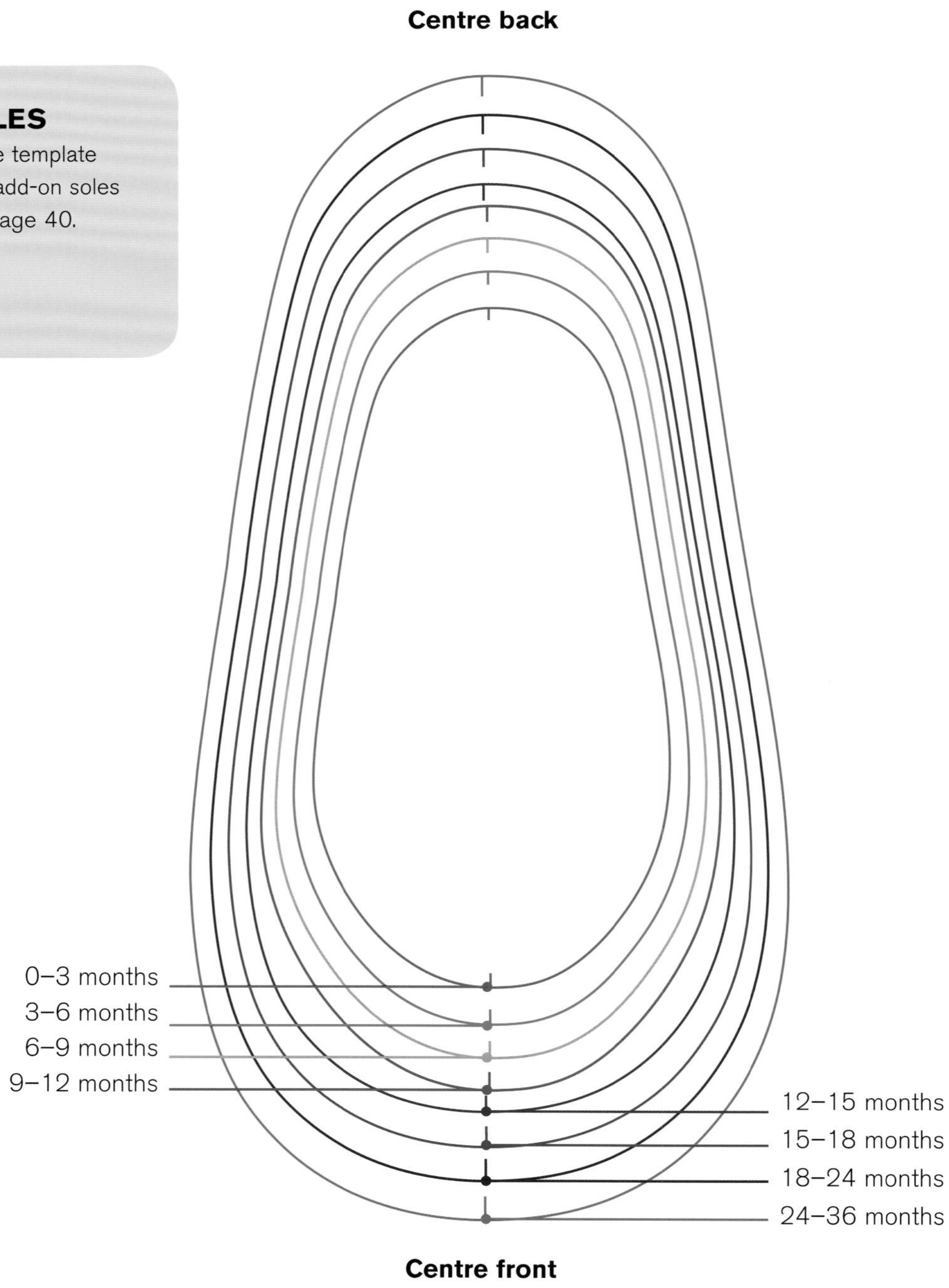

Centre back

0–3 months
3–6 months
6–9 months
9–12 months

12–15 months
15–18 months
18–24 months
24–36 months

Centre front

Ankle Tie Shoes
(see page 29)

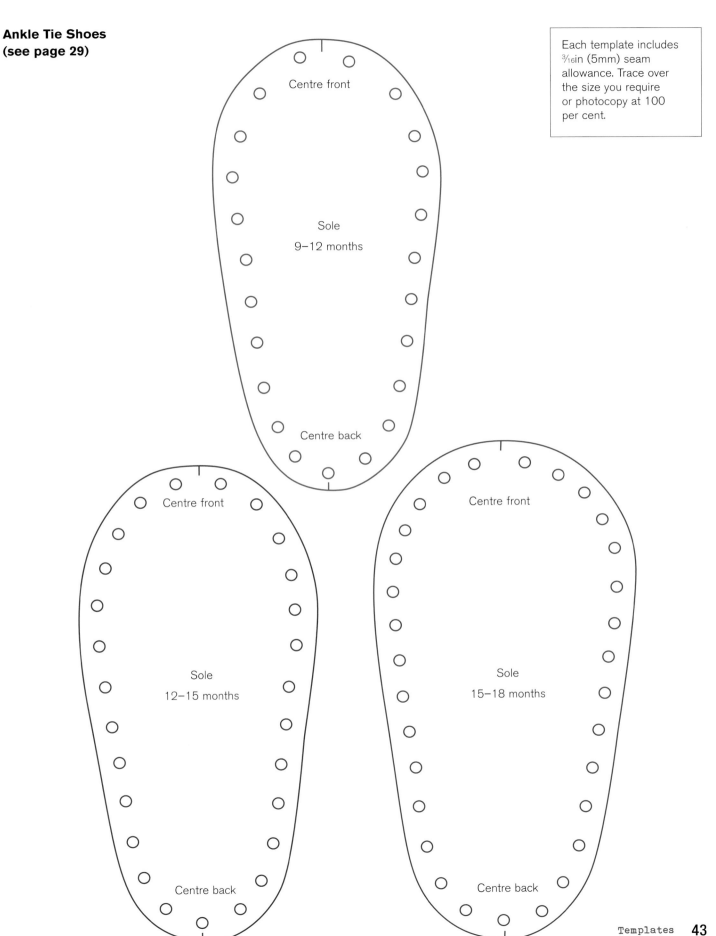

Centre front

Sole
9–12 months

Centre back

Each template includes
³⁄₁₆in (5mm) seam
allowance. Trace over
the size you require
or photocopy at 100
per cent.

Centre front

Sole
12–15 months

Centre back

Centre front

Sole
15–18 months

Centre back

Each template includes ³⁄₁₆in (5mm) seam allowance. Trace over the size you require or photocopy at 100 per cent.

**Strappy Sandals
(see page 32)**

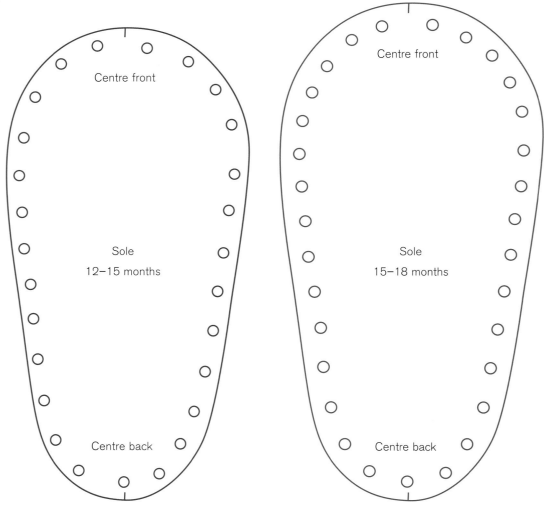

Centre front

Sole
12–15 months

Centre back

Centre front

Sole
15–18 months

Centre back

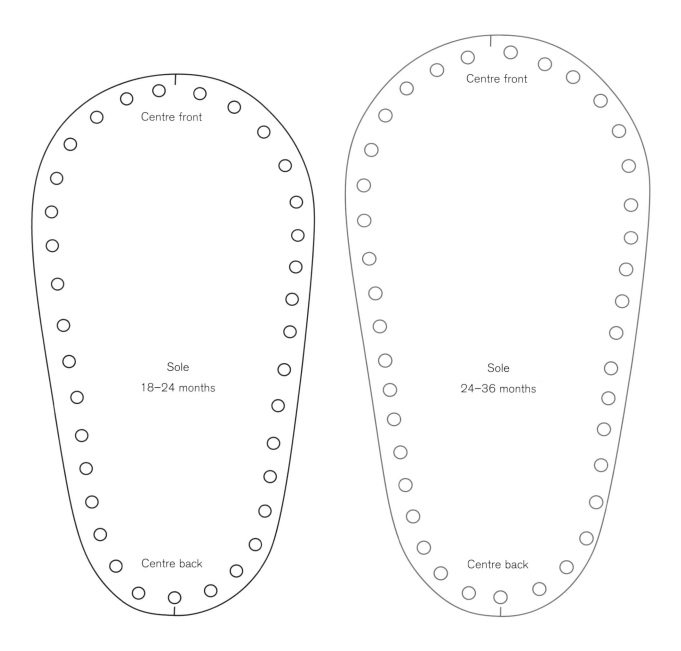

Centre front

Sole
18–24 months

Centre back

Centre front

Sole
24–36 months

Centre back

Daisy Slippers
(see page 22)

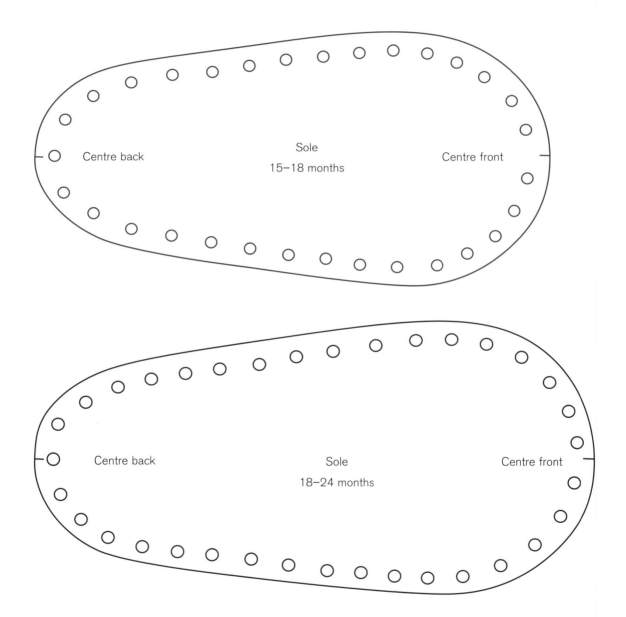

Centre back   Sole   Centre front
15–18 months

Centre back   Sole   Centre front
18–24 months

Each template includes
³⁄₁₆in (5mm) seam
allowance. Trace over
the size you require
or photocopy it at 100
per cent.

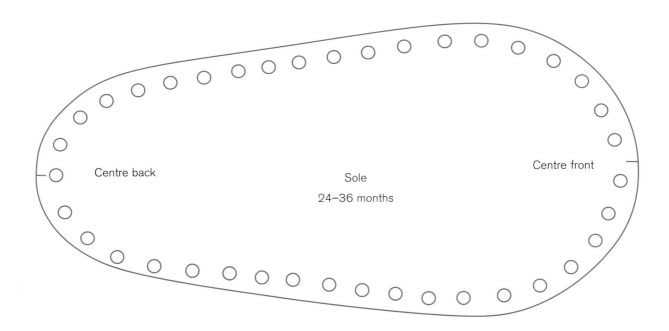

Centre back

Sole

24–36 months

Centre front

Abbreviations

beg	begin(ning)	**mm**	millimetre(s)
ch	chain	**prev**	previous
ch sp	chain space	**rem**	remaining
cm	centimetre(s)	**rep**	repeat
dc	double crochet (US: single crochet)	**RS**	right side
dc2tog	work 2 double crochet together over next two stitches (decrease by 1 stitch)	**sl st**	slip stitch
		sp	space
dtr	double treble (US: triple)	**st**	stitch
g	gram(s)	**tr**	treble (US: double crochet)
htr	half treble (US: half double crochet)	**WS**	wrong side
htr4tog	work 4 half treble together over next four stitches (decrease by 3 stitches)	*****	work instructions immediately following *, then repeat as directed
in	inch(es)	**( )**	repeat instructions inside brackets as many times as instructed
m	metre(s)		

Conversions

CROCHET HOOKS

UK	Metric	US
14	2mm	–
13	2.25mm	B-1
12	2.5mm	–
–	2.75mm	C-2
11	3mm	–
10	3.25mm	D-3
9	3.5mm	E-4
–	3.75mm	F-5
8	4mm	G-6
7	4mm	7
6	5mm	H-8
5	5mm	I-9
4	6mm	J-10
3	6mm	K-10.5
2	7mm	–
0	8mm	L-11
00	9mm	M–N-13
000	10mm	N–P-15

UK/US CROCHET TERMS

UK	US
Double crochet	Single crochet
Half treble	Half double crochet
Treble	Double crochet
Double treble	Triple crochet
Treble treble	Double triple crochet

UK/US YARN WEIGHTS

UK	US
2-ply	Lace
3-ply	Fingering
4-ply	Sport
DK (double knitting)	Light worsted
Aran	Fisherman/worsted
Chunky	Bulky
Super chunky	Extra bulky

Other booklets include:

ISBN: 978-1-78494-168-0

ISBN: 978-1-78494-165-9

ISBN: 978-1-78494-160-4

ISBN: 978-1-78494-162-8

ISBN: 978-1-78494-164-2

ISBN: 978-1-78494-462-9

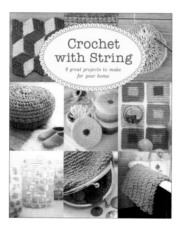

ISBN: 978-1-78494-461-2

ISBN: 978-1-78494-463-6

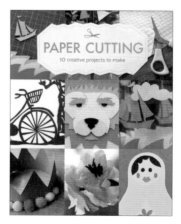

ISBN: 978-1-78494-464-3

To place an order, or to request a catalogue, contact:
GMC Publications Ltd
166 High Street, Lewes, East Sussex, BN7 1XU, United Kingdom
Tel: + 44 (0)1273 488005 • www.gmcbooks.com

A new baby or toddler is the perfect excuse to get creative, and a handmade pair of crocheted booties or slippers makes a delightful gift. This adorable collection of 10 projects is packed full of gorgeous designs to keep tiny toes warm. With handy templates and all the basic know-how presented in a clearly explained step-by-step format, there's everything you need to get started.

£5.99   US$9.95

ISBN 978-1-78494-460-5

9 781784 944605

www.gmcbooks.com